MY BIBLE stories
Activity Book

Turn the page to discover inspirational
Bible stories and charming puzzles and activities.

•

Then press-out the card pages
to create some adorable Bible-themed crafts.

•

You can use your shiny stickers in the book, to finish
your crafts, or wherever else you want!

make
believe
ideas

WUNDERFUL WURLD

God made the world. He made the sun, earth, and sky.
Color the picture. Use the key to guide you.

God made the nighttime. He made the moon and the stars.

1

6

7

7

7

4

4

4

6

8

6

8

8

6

6

5

3

3

2

5

3

5

3

3

Find the animals that match these shapes.

7

JUNGLE RUMBLE

God made all the animals, from giant elephants to tiny mice.
Search the jungle for the animals below.

How many can you see?
Write the answers in the circles.

tigers **1**

elephants

monkeys

chameleons ....   toucans ....   mice ....

GARDEN OF EDEN

God made Adam and Eve. He put them in a lovely garden called Eden.
Find and circle eight differences between the scenes.

① ② ③ ④ ⑤ ⑥ ⑦ ⑧

FORBIDDEN FRUIT

A sly snake tempted Adam and Eve to eat fruit from God's forbidden tree.
Circle **true** for things that are in the picture.
Circle **false** for things that are not in the picture.

There are three forbidden apples on the tree.	True	False
The sly snake is orange.	True	False
Eve is holding an apple.	True	False

BUILD THE ARK

God told Noah to build a big wooden boat called an ark.
Join the dots to finish Noah's ark. Then finish coloring the picture.

Search the page for the following things.

2 hammers ☐

3 nails ☐

5 planks ☐

TWO BY TWO

Noah took two of every animal into the ark.
Use color to make the animal pairs match.

9

STORMY SEH

God made it rain for 40 days and nights until the Earth was covered in water. Guide the ark through the stormy sea to reach dry land.

Start →

Finish

KHINBOW SEHKCH

God sent a rainbow as a promise that He would not flood the earth again. Search the grid for the rainbow colors. Words can go across or down.

red	orange	yellow	green

blue	indigo	violet

g	q	y	p	i	n	d	i	g	o
r	e	d	r	k	u	v	c	h	a
e	b	n	b	t	f	i	s	d	m
e	j	b	r	m	b	q	z	o	n
n	y	j	x	c	l	k	e	r	b
q	g	l	t	l	u	w	g	a	w
p	v	i	o	l	e	t	l	n	r
h	a	e	c	g	k	h	q	g	b
o	z	m	v	k	m	u	v	e	l
s	y	e	l	l	o	w	d	o	f

11

COLORFUL COAT

Jacob gave a special coat of many colors to his favorite son, Joseph.
Guide Joseph through the maze to find his colored coat.
Try to pass his 11 jealous brothers along the way.

BY THE RIVER

An Egyptian princess found baby Moses in a basket by a river.
Color the picture. Use the dots to guide you.

Search the picture for the hidden letters
and unscramble them to reveal a name. ....

15

BURNING BUSH

God spoke to Moses from a burning bush.
Which path adds up to the biggest number?
Write the answer.

....

Finish

Start

A   B   C

1   1   1   2   2   2

PARTING THE SEA

God helped Moses to part the sea and lead His people out of Egypt. Help Moses' people cross the seabed. Use the key to guide you.

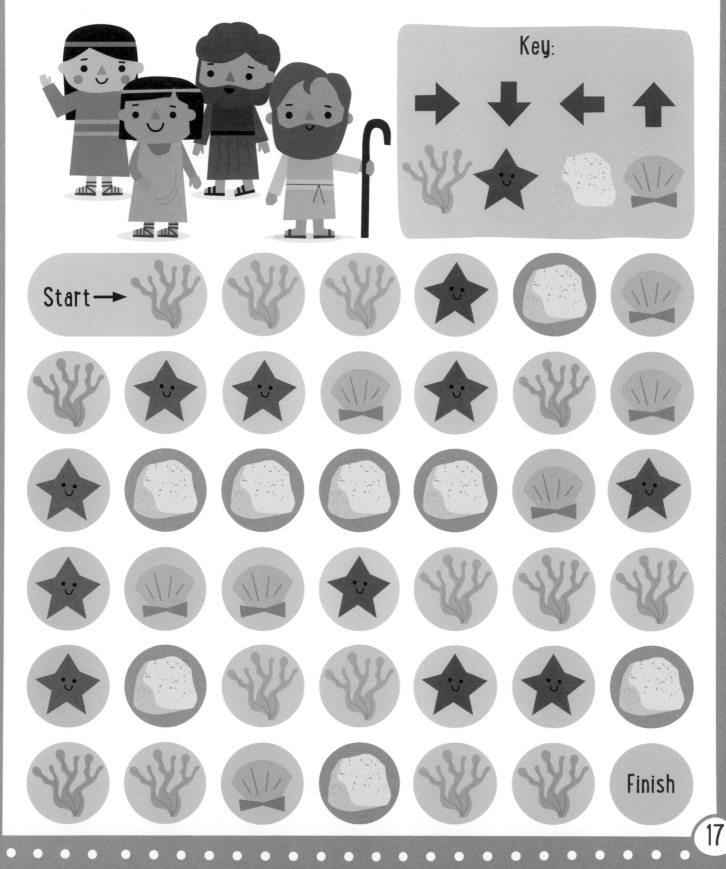

DAVID FIGHTS GOLIATH

David was a brave shepherd boy who
fought against the giant Goliath.

Which square doesn't belong in this picture? Write the letter.

A B C D

God helped David to win the fight.
David hit Goliath with a stone and the giant fell.
Unscramble the words. Use the pictures as a guide.

D i a v d

t l a G i h o

How many objects can you count in each section?
Write the answers in the circles.

.... slingshots

.... shields

LIONS' DEN

God kept Daniel safe in the lions' den.
Trace the lines to finish the picture. Then color it.

Circle the smallest lion.

SEA SEARCH

Jonah prayed to God to save him from a big whale. Use the grid to finish the quiz. First, read the letter, and then read the number.

For example, the jellyfish is in E2.

Is Jonah in B4?

Yes No

Is there a lightning bolt in E7?

Yes No

Is the whale in A1?

Yes No

Which square is the anchor in? Write the answer.

....

Which square is the seahorse in? Write the answer.

....

What is in E3?

boat

fish

storm cloud

jellyfish

turtle

23

JUUKNEY TU BETHLEHEM

An angel told Mary she was having a baby. He would be the Son of God.
Guide Mary and Joseph to Bethlehem without touching the sides.

Start

Finish

JESUS IS BORN

Mary gave birth to Jesus in a stable.
Color the segments to complete the picture.

GOOD NEWS

Angels appeared to some shepherds and told them to visit Jesus. Search the scene for the objects below. Color one box for each object.

star	angels	shepherds	trees	sheep

GREAT GIFTS

Three wise men followed a bright star and brought gifts to Jesus. Follow the lines to see each gift. Write the letters in the circles.

A gold

B frankincense

C myrrh

WORD OF GOD

Five thousand people came to hear Jesus speak about God's Word. Use color to finish the picture.

LOAVES AND FISH

Jesus performed a miracle. He fed the crowd with only a few loaves and fish.
Are there more loaves or fish? Write the totals in the circles.

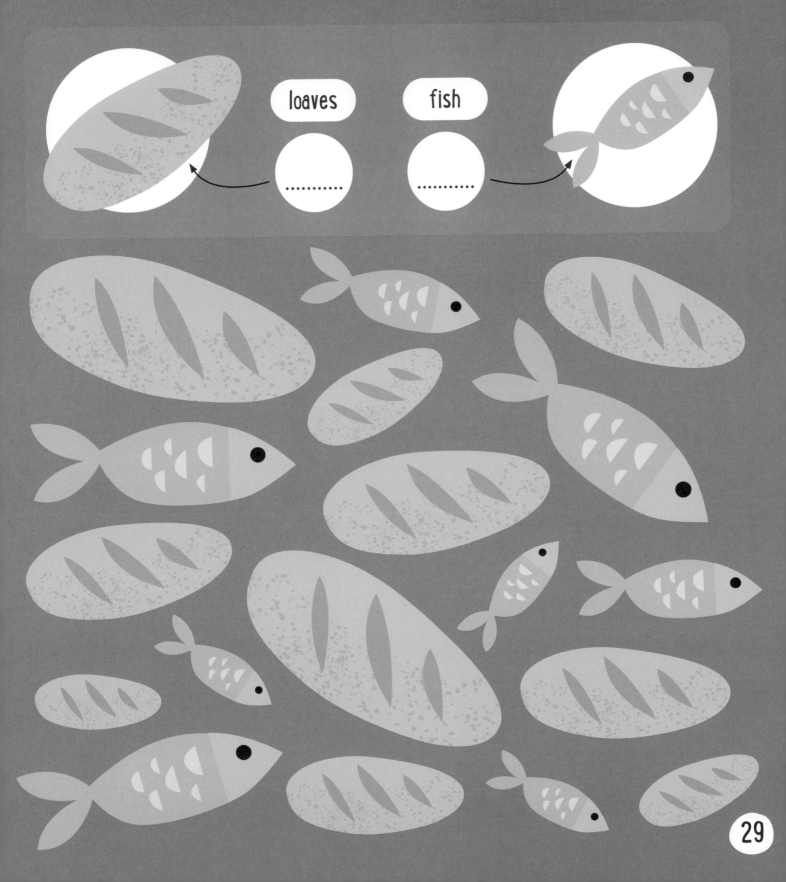

loaves

fish

A HELPING HAND

A man was robbed and left hurt on the road. Check the box next to the good Samaritan who reaches the middle and helps the hurt man.

Finish

THE GOOD SHMARITAN

Write the correct letter in each box to match the missing pieces to their sections.

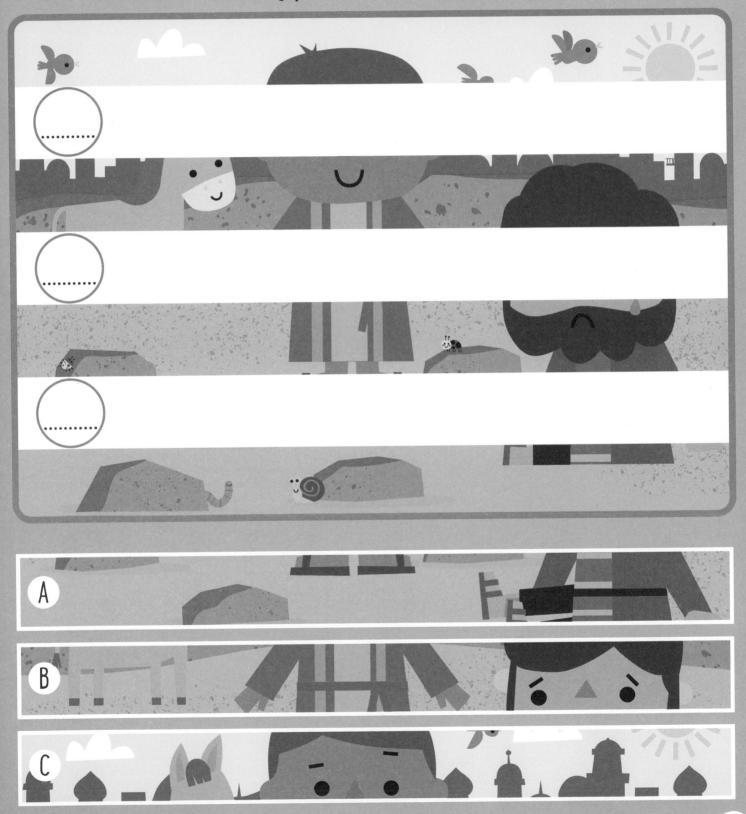

EASTER CELEBRATION

Jesus died on a cross to save us. He rose again after three days. Draw a picture of something you love about Easter. Then use color to finish it.

GARDEN OF EDEN

On the next two pages, you will find everything you need to create a Garden of Eden scene.

1. Press out the garden scene and stands.
2. Slot the garden scene into the stands to finish.

stands

1 Press out the models and stands.
2 Then slot the stands into each model.
3 Slot the snake onto the apple tree.

NOAH'S ANIMAL PAIRS

How to play:

1 Press out the cards and arrange them facedown in the play area.

2 Take turns choosing two cards and turning them faceup. If the cards match, keep the pair. If they do not match, turn them back over.

3 Keep playing until you have found all the pairs. The winner is the player with the most pairs at the end.

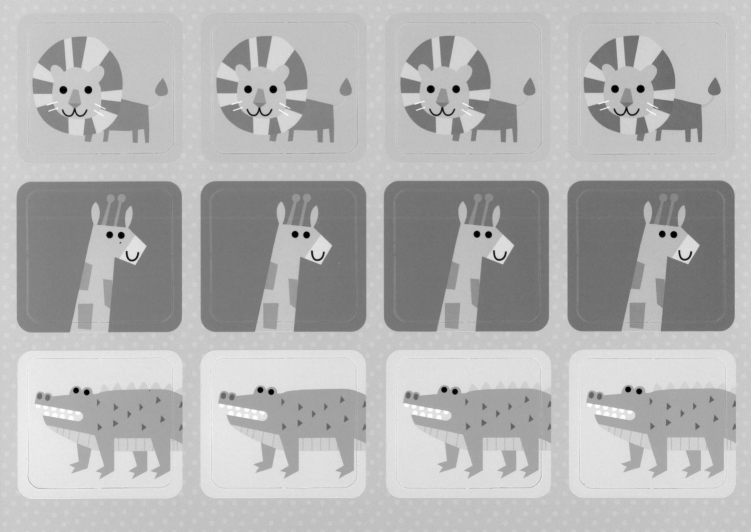

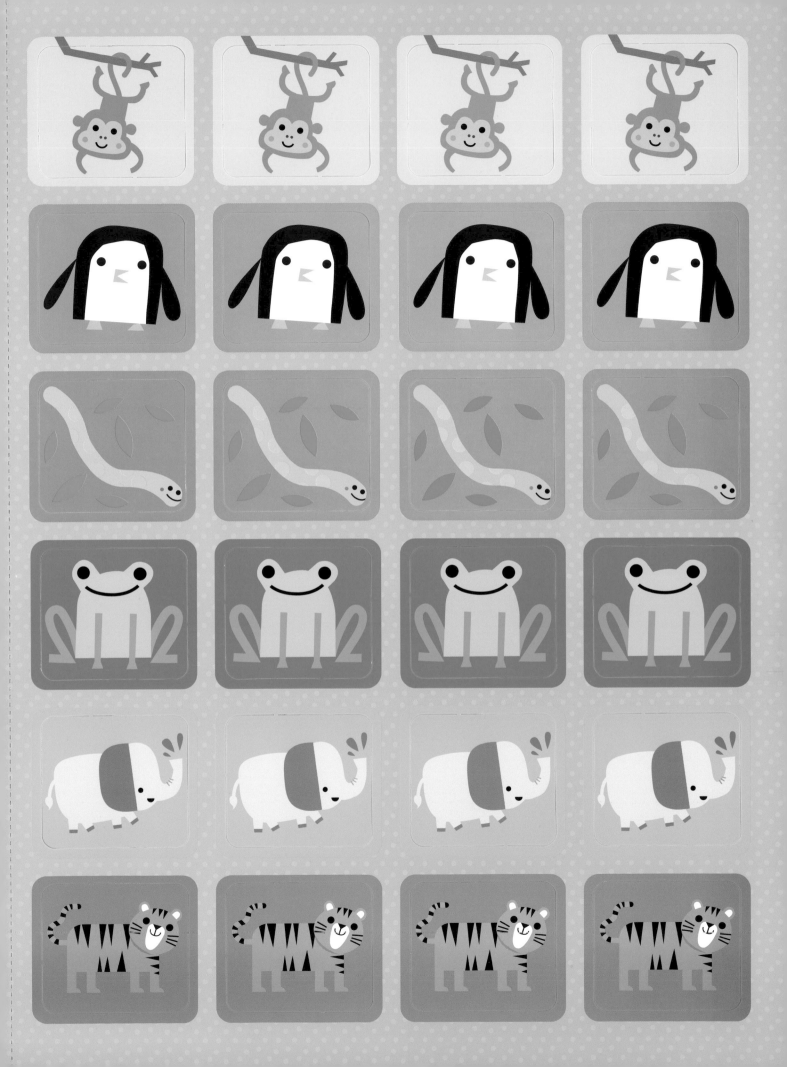

JOSEPH'S JIGSAW

1. Press out the puzzle pieces and mix them up.
2. Then put the pieces back together to make this picture.

LOAVES AND FISH

How to play:

1 Press out the game board and counters.

2 Give one player the loaf counters and one player the fish counters.

3 Take turns putting a counter on the board. The first player to get three of their counters in a row wins!

This is a game for 2 players.

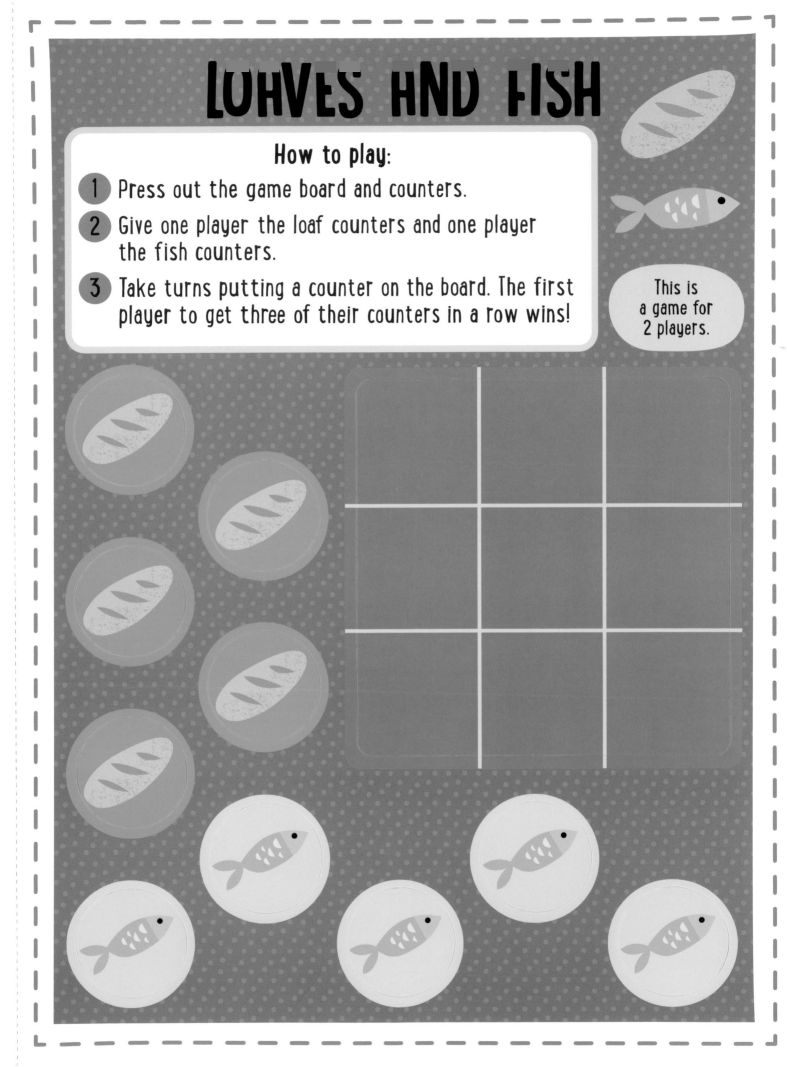

DAVID'S SHEEP

Press out the sheep mask, eye holes, and small holes either side.
Then ask an adult to help you thread some ribbon through
the small holes and tie it around your head.

ROAR-SOME PUPPET

1 Gently press out the puppet and handles.

2 Fold the puppet along the creases.

3 Glue the ends of the handles onto the back of the puppet.

4 Slide your hand into the puppet handles, then open and close your hand to roar like a lion!

handles

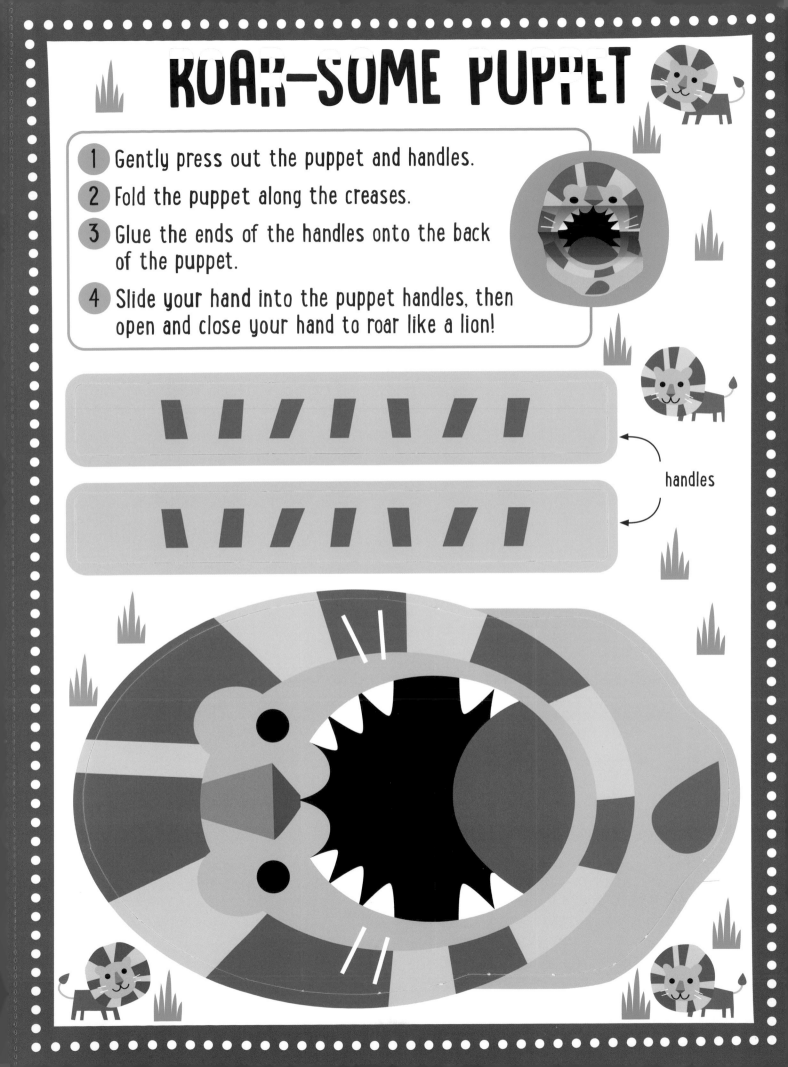